The Color Book

Volume One

Legal Stuff

Copyright @ 1995-2006 by The Fashiondex, Inc. All rights reserved. No part of this book may be reproduced or transmitted in any form or by any means, including but not limited to mechanical, electronic, photocopying, or any information storage or retrieval system, without the prior written permission of The Fashiondex, Inc.

The Fashiondex, Inc. cannot accept responsibility for the accuracy or completeness of information contained herein, or for loss or damage caused by any use thereof.

Book design, cover design, logo artwork, text and format owned by The Fashiondex, Inc.

All inquiries should be directed to:
The Fashiondex, Inc.
153 West 27th Street,
New York, NY 10001
info@fashiondex.com

Printed in the United States of America.
First printing 1995.
Second printing 1996.
Third printing 1997.
Fourth printing 1998.
Fifth printing 1999.
Sixth printing 2001.
Seventh printing 2003.
ISBN 09714867-1-9

Intro

We all know the time and brainpower it takes to name your colors each season. It's a fun job, but sometimes frustrating and usually uses a big chunk of time that you could be using for another task.

With this in mind, we designed The Color Book to help you name your colors as quickly as possible, but retain the level of creativity and fun always associated with the job. Here are over 1,300 color names for you to pick and choose from, all arranged by hue.

No longer need you fret on what to call your Dark Green this holiday season, now you can just go to the book, look behind the Green Page and just choose "Mistletoe"! It's fun, fast and easy.

We hope this book makes your job easier, saves you time and inspires you. Because, we at Fashiondex work everyday to save designer's time and make your lives easier.

Thank you for your purchase, and as always, our support staff at 914 271 6121 is ready to answer your questions and take suggestions and comments at all times- so we can make The Fashiondex books and The Color Book even more useful to you.

Sincerely,

The Fashiondex Inc.

White

Bleach

Snow

Cloud

Chalk

Ice

Bianco

Talc

Quartz

Eggshell

Snowball

Plaster

Winter

White

White

Glacier

Ghost

Snowflake

Arrowroot

Icicle

Camellia

Gardenia

Cottonball

Marshmallow

Milk White

Porcelain

Enamel

Eggwhite

Bridal Veil

Coconut

Snowstone

Gladiola

Magnolia

Albino

Aurora

Comet

Snow White

Igloo

Unicorn

Swan

Lead White

White

White

Starch White

Tennis White

Sneaker

Seasalt

Purity

Virgin White

Snowbell

Optic White

Bleach White

Diamond

Snow Bunny

Pure White

Crystalline

Ozark White

Froth

Solar White

Blanc

Apollo

Titanium

Cottontail

Bunny

Polar Bear

Arctic

White

Ivory

Vanilla

Pearl

Antique white

Off-white

Cream

Canvas

Linen

Bone

Crystal

Lace

Opal

Buttermilk

Candle

Ivory

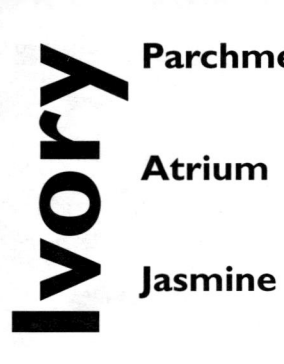

Parchment

Atrium

Jasmine

Tusk

Creamware

Vanilla Bean

Stucco

Glaze

Alabaster

China Doll

Farina

White Sand

Creamora

Bone China

Rock Candy

Oyster

Navajo White

Horseradish

Whipped Cream

Creampuff

Pumice

Milky Way

Gypsum

Aged

Ivory

Natural

Sandrock

Beige

Nude

Bisque

Putty

Barley

Sand

Old Lace

Almond

Tanstone

Sandstone

Neutral

Natural

Natural

Sawdust

Beach

Mojavi

Flax

Hemp

Hay

Raffia

Oatmeal

Ramie

Rope

Ecru

Wicker

Oat

Natural

Muslin

Bamboo

Natura

Sahara

Rock

Ale

Balsam

Tortilla

Bean Sprout

Wheat

Alfalfa

Straw

Rattan

Natural

Jute

Oak

Dune

Wheat Germ

Shetland

Sanddrift

Khaki

Sanddune

Beachwood

Boardwalk

Hummus

Grain

Natural

Fossil

Moonrock

Millstone

Tallow

Milkweed

Sandbox

Hacienda

Burlap

Hominy

Desert Sand

Camel

Chamois

Beeswax

Ash Blonde

Chanterelle

Chardonnay

Zinfandel

Blonde

Butter

Ginger

Safflower

Camel

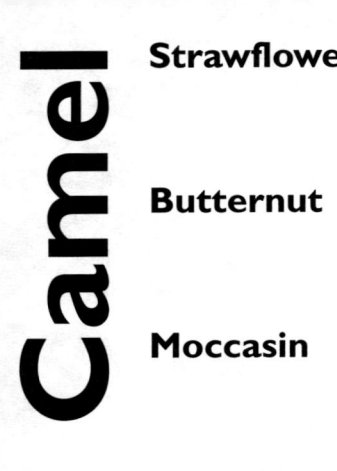

Strawflower

Butternut

Moccasin

Moonlight

Candlelight

Manilla

India

Husk

Champagne

Sauterne

Candelabra

Corncob

Cornmeal

Custard

Eggnog

Applesauce

Buttercream

Aztec Clay

Camel

Pale Yellow

Banana

Daffodil

Buttercup

Eggcream

Sun

Squash

Sunrise

Flaxen

Meringue

Mellow

Shimmer

Sundrop

Lemonade

Chamomille

Pale Yellow

Angelhair

Daydream

Daylily

Hollandaise

Bernaise

Lemon Sorbet

Banana Cream

Lumina

Plantain

Sol

Baby Chick

Yellow

Lemon

Yellow

Spotlight

Sunflower

Daisy

Marigold

Grapefruit

Dandelion

Sunspot

Citrus

Sunlight

Taxicab

Cadmium

Yellow

Sunshine

Zest

Angelfish

Slicker

Lemon Rind

Bumble Bee

Lemon Twist

Sunfish

Canary

Freesia

Jonquil

Calendula

Solar

Yellowstone

Citronella

Neon

Chrome Yellow

Pineapple

Sunburst

Flourescent

Sulfur

Citrine

Egg Yolk

Safety Yellow

Yellow

Gold

Clarion

Topaz

Honey

Sunset

Sap

Cheddar

Corn

Yellow gold

Goldfish

Saffron

Maize

Ochre

Aztec

Gold

Gold

Inca

Harvest

Karat

Cumin

Gold Rush

Pollen

Cyanide

Mustard

Dijon

Curry

Amber

Coronation

Gold Plate

Sassafras

Gold

Honeycomb

Honeysuckle

Forsythia

Nugget

Crown Gold

Midas Touch

Oro

Glitter

Gold Mine

Spun Gold

Indian Yellow

Goldenrod

Peach

Prawn

Flesh

Melon

Mango

Apricot

Scallops

Soapstone

Sorbet

Parfait

Sherbert

Cantaloupe

Peach Mousse

Bermuda

Cameo

Peachblossom

Peach

Orange

Papaya

Poppy

Tangerine

Torrid

Zinnia

Mandarine

Tropicana

Firefly

Flash

Nuclear

Nectar

Orangeade

Orange

Orange

Kumquat

Carrot

Nectarine

Tangelo

Tiger

Sweet Potato

Clementine

Crush

Guava

Yam

Cosmo

Day-Glo

Salamander

Torch

Pumpkin

Passionfruit

Popsicle

Navel

Bittersweet

Persimmon

Pulp

Jellybean

Ember

O.J.

Orange

Coral

Shrimp

Salmon

Calypso

Primrose

Flamingo

Sunburn

Rhubarb

Ocean Coral

Geranium

Coral Ice

Coral Reef

Watermelon

Coral

Pink

Pink

Petal

Shell

Powder

Petticoat

Puff

Whisper

Blush

Ballet

Bare

Pale Pink

Tutu

Carnation

Candy

Pink

Rose Quartz

Sugar Pink

Pearl Pink

Candy Pink

Cottage Pink

China pink

Cotton Candy

Pink Lemonade

Pink Chiffon

Bouquet

Ribbon

Rosebud

Dauphine

Innocence

Cattleya

Cosmetic

Hint

Barely Pink

Sappho

Afterglow

Blossom

Seashell

Pink Lady

Pink Grapefruit

Baby's Breath

Chrysanthemum

Dutch Pink

Maiden Pink

Pink

Hot Pink

Tulip

Azalea

Cerise

Fuchsia

Camilla

Shocking Pink

Electric Pink

Bubble Gum

Fiesta

Hibiscus

Lotus

Hot Pink

Hot Pink

Punch

Wild Rose

Primrose

Shocking

Hydrangea

Begonia

Petunia

Magenta

Garland

Red

Ruby

Garnet

Flame

Cherry

Berry

Raspberry

Crimson

Cranberry

Lipstick

Ladybug

Lolipop

Cardinal

Heartbeat

Red

Red

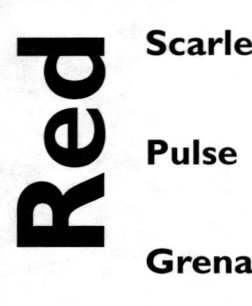

Scarlet

Pulse

Grenadine

Bing Cherry

Fruit Punch

Hot Rod

Fire

Target

Bombshell

Cherrystone

Beet

Hellfire

Stoplight

Rocket

Red

Salsa

Snapper

Venetian Red

Bloodred

Strawberry

Wagon Red

Anger

Pimento

Radish

Radioactive

Pommegrante

Poinsetta

Lacquer

Red Fox

Red

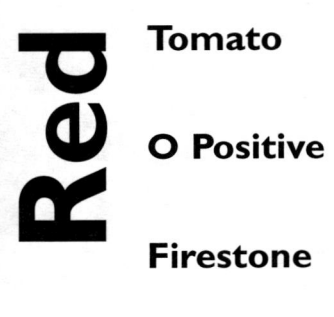

Tomato

O Positive

Firestone

Fire Engine

Vermillion

Heartbreak

Firecracker

Jalapeno

Minium

Amaryllis

Rubescent

Cranapple

Cassis

Crab

Red

Candied Apple

Hot Lips

Bloodshot

Wild Cherry

Devil

Cambridge Red

Simply Red

Hot Red

Crayfish

Hot Tamale

Redhot

TNT

Mars Red

Rose

Rose

Rosetta

Rosebud

Mauve

Rouge

Tearose

Rosewood

Primrose

English Rose

Sweetbrier

Desert Rose

Rose

Rosemist

Colonial Rose

Terra Rosa

Rosewater

Dusty Rose

Rose Ash

Rosetone

Old Rose

Lavendar

Lilac

Thistle

Orchid

Iris

Squill

Heather

Violet

Posy

Hyacinth

Heliotrope

Lavendar

Lavendar

Purple Sage

Frosted Plum

Viola

Purple Haze

Ophelia

Wisteria

Dusty Lilac

Dahlia

Purple

Passion

Grape

Pansy

Delphinium

Amethyst

Aubergine

Cardoon

Huckleberry

Damask

Plum

Borage

Concord

Purple

Purple

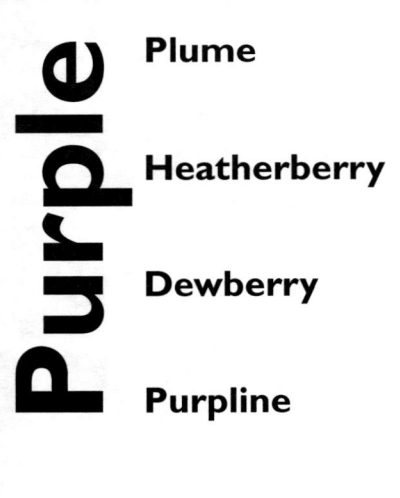

Plume

Heatherberry

Dewberry

Purpline

Jelly

Eminence

Blue Violet

Passionflower

Magenta

Valor

Damson

Deep Purple

Eggplant

Raisin

Prune

Mulberry

Blackberry

Gooseberry

Hollyhock

Bramble

Bayberry

Rum Raisin

Razzleberry

Pale Blue

Pond

Sky

Rain

Mist

Glacier

Bluestar

Bluebell

Bonnet

Meadow

Meteor

Pale Blue

Pale Blue

Blue Opal

Heather

Horizon

Baby Blue

Sweet William

Humility

Lake

Porcelain Blue

Iceberg

Wedgewood

Antique Blue

Pale Blue

Mystic Blue

Crystal Blue

French Blue

Frost Blue

Space Blue

Blueblossom

Bluebird

Cornflower

Constellation

Celestial Blue

Robin's Egg

Pale Blue

Dolphin

Alpine Blue

Chambray

Breeze

Dewdrop

Powder Blue

Placid

Blue

Royal

Marine

Sapphire

Cobalt

Cadet

Bridgewater

Periwinkle

Flag Blue

Bluefish

Copen

Blue

Blue

Cyan

Tile Blue

China Blue

Bluejay

Aztec Blue

Lapis

Cerulean

Ultramarine

Electric Blue

Century Blue

South Pacific

Mediteranean

Nile Blue

Bluestone

Blueberry

Blue Danube

Bluebeard

Pool

Tidal

Blue Bayou

Blue

Denim

Denim

Dungaree

Slate Blue

Blue Corn

Mayflower

Steel Blue

Stonewash

Sandwash

Chambray

Petrol

Workshirt

Blue Collar

Blue Heron

Methyl Blue

Quaker Blue

Blue Fox

Navy

Ink

Indigo

Carbon

Midnight Blue

Old Navy

Federal Blue

Prussian Blue

Gettysgurg

Normandy Blue

Corporate Blue

Yankee

Officer's Blue

Galaxy Blue

Navy

Aqua

Azure

Seamist

Seafoam

Island

Seaspray

Neptune

Atlantis

Ocean

Zenith

Seabreeze

Aquashell

Capri

Aqua

Aqua

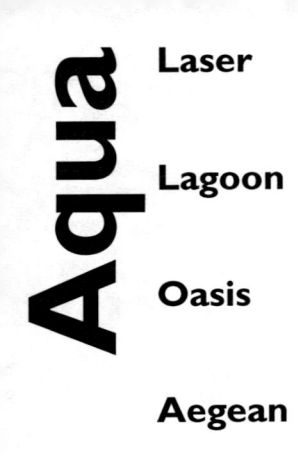

Laser

Lagoon

Oasis

Aegean

Atlantic

Tropic

Kingfisher

Turquoise

Seafrost

Cayman

Cancun

Pacific

Seaside

Coast

Nautica

Aquarium

Aquatint

Caribe

Canard

Aquamarine

Tide

Sea Green

Sea

Spray

H$_2$O

Oceanstorm

Aqua

Teal

Teal

Jade

Mallard

Bottle Green

Bluegrass

Peacock

Jasper

Deep Aqua

Malachite

Deep Sea

Pale Green

Pale Green

Mint

Kiwi

Snapdragon

Celadon

Moss

Keylime

Lettuce

Willow

Pear

Aloe

Eucalyptus

Celery

Spearmint

Apple

Pale Green

Mineral

Avocado

Quince

Cucumber

Lemongrass

Wintergreen

Honeydew

Melonball

Pistachio

Fairy Green

Escarole

Glowworm

Tamale

Absinthe

Green

Green

Grass

Palm

Kelly

Parrot

Peppermint

Zucchini

Parsley

Leaf Green

Chrome Green

Grasshopper

Vine

Green

Artichoke

Turtle

Sweet Pea

Clover

Margarita

Stinger

Creme de Menthe

Watercress

Shamrock

Midori

Sprout

Limeade

Green

Iguana

Leprechaun

Lizard

Kermit

Cricket

Tree

Envy

Palmetto

Parakeet

Asparagus

Green Bean

Verte

Green

Serpent

Viridian

Jealousy

Broccoli

Emerald

Lime

Spinach

Scallion

Cryptonite

Chartreuse

Oxide Green

Neon Green

Citrine

Acid

Rainforrest

Tile Green

Pasture

Bellpepper

Frog

Green Acres

Guacamole

Green

Dark Green

Hunter

Spruce

Forrest

Fir

Pine

Holly

Cypress

Evergreen

Hemlock

Myrtle

Dark Green

Jungle

Juniper

Christmas Tree

Wreath

Elm

Everglade

Sherwood

Mistletoe

Fern

Sage

Dill

Rosemary

Ivyland

Sorrel

Patina

Pesto

Basil

Cactus

Seaweed

Cilantro

Chervil

Herb

Fern

Fern

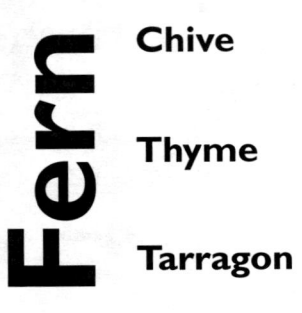

- Chive
- Thyme
- Tarragon
- Ivy
- Sagebrush
- Frond
- Bay Leaf
- Acanthus
- Foliage Green
- Vineyard
- Herbal

Olive

Woodland

Sprig

Loden

Laurel

Reed

Safari

Olive Drab

Pickle

Army Green

Arugula

Crocodile

O.D.

Olive Branch

Surgical Scrubs

Copper

Copper

Bronze

Chestnut

Penny

Sienna

Auburn

Butterscotch

Brown Sugar

Caramel

Brass

Cider

Satay

Copper

Turbinado

Pueblo

Praline

Turmeric

Tawny

Ginseng

Gingersnap

Gingerbread

Brandy

Copperplate

Autumn Gold

Cinnamon

Cedar

Sienna

Sierra

Spice

Cinnabar

Burnish

Rum

Terracotta

Cardamon

Rustic

Amaretto

Autumn Leaf

Bismarcck

Cinnamon

Cinnamon

Syrup

Henna

Auburn

Terrazzo

Rancho

Maple

Sherry

Sepia

Burnt Sienna

Pompeii

Hot Pepper

Peppercorn

Pepper

Rust

Clay

Chili

Russet

Firethorn

Paprika

Coriander

Cayenne

Tabasco

Crabapple

Pepper

Pepper

Fireeater

Bloody Maria

Adobe

Claypot

Pepperoni

Chipolte

Fireside Orange

Pumpkin

Brick

Henna

Blood

Indian Red

Redwood

Sequoia

Bleeding Heart

Barn Red

Briquet

Cherrywood

Red Oak

Redrock

Maple

Navajo Red

Ranchhouse Red

Brick

Wine

Wine

Plum

Rose'

Burgundy

Bloodstone

Port

Currant

Bordeaux

Fig

Elderberry

Maroon

Merlot

Sangria

Vintage

Madder

wine

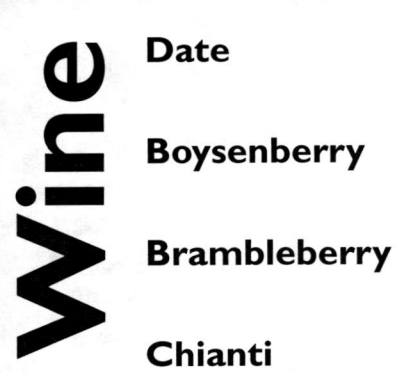

Date

Boysenberry

Brambleberry

Chianti

Beaujolais

Madeira

Rubine

Claret

Dubonnet

Cabernet

Kir

Sanquine

Allspice

Sultan

Black Cherry

Wine

Carmine

Byzantine Red

Blackcurrant

Acacia

Wineberry

Ruddy

Winterberry

Red Jasper

Oxblood

Red Earth

Burnt Rose

Chambord

Black Raspberry

Lingonberry

Raddichio

Taupe

Taupe

Beech

Bark

Driftwood

Stone

Malt

Mushroom

Tan

Rye

Truffle

Barley

Flagstone

Nomad

Pebblestone

Taupe

French Almond

Lager

Prarie

Suntan

Whiskey

Irish Cream

French Taupe

Tea

Pekoe

Flintstone

Woodsage

Toast

Fawn

Doe

Peanut

Acorn

Tuscany

Light Brown

Buckwheat

Caraway

Toffee

Saddleback

Umber

Luggage

Pecan

Anteloupe

Fawn

Fawn

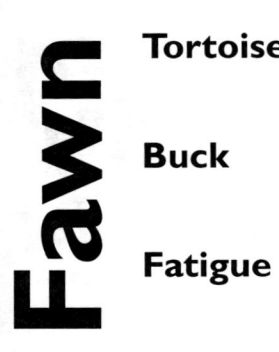

Tortoise

Buck

Fatigue

Weather

Antler

Sheepskin

Doeskin

Navajo

Santa Fe

Nut Crunch

Pale Ale

Woodchip

Musk

Buckskin

Fawn

Leather

Suede

Nu-buck

Sycamore

Noisette

Gazelle

Oregano

Pigskin

Woodruff

Carton

Tootsie Roll

Cafe Au Lait

Sepia

Bran

Fawn

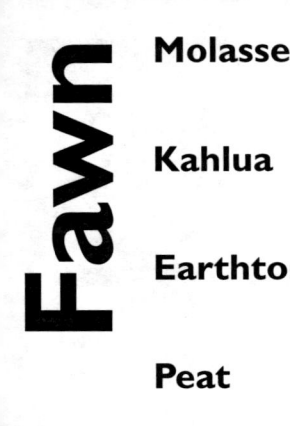

Molasses

Kahlua

Earthtone

Peat

Dogwood

Jicama

Branch

Hearthstone

Twig

Raw Umber

Canyon Brown

Brown

Brown

Teak

Mulch

Wood

Java

Earth

Mocha

Cola

Rootbeer

Carob

Tobacco

Mink

Teddy Bear

Muskrat

Nut

Brown

Mesa Brown

Cognac

Wrangler

Coffee Bean

Brunette

Tobac

Spanish Brown

Thoroughbred

Bronco

Saddle

Sasparilla

Ponderosa

Mud

Palomino

Sumac

Brown

Buffalo

Beaver

Mudslide

Mesquite

Pinecone

Hazel

Brownstone

Peanut Brittle

Fresh Roast

Clove

Burel

Peppercorn

Decaf

Cocoa

Cappucino

Brown

Nutmeg

Chicory

Chocolate Malt

Fudge

Hazelnut

Mud Pie

Birch Beer

Brindle

Coffee

Burnt Umber

Puce

Birch

Sludge Brown

Dark Brown

Deep Brown

Walnut

Mahogany

Espresso

Chocolate

Pumpernickel

Sable

Bison

Cordovan

Condor

Dark Brown

Dark Brown

Mustang

Hickory

Havana

Snuff

Seal Brown

Velvet Brown

Mochachino

Van Dyke Brown

Pale Grey

Dove

Fog

Platinum

Ash

Cloud

Pearl Grey

Pebble

Cement

Chrome

Spur

Nickel

Tin

Dusk

Silverbell

Pale Grey

Pale Grey

Moonshine

Drizzle

Pelican

Ice Gray

Tombstone

Agate

Moonbeam

Moonlit

Luna

Stainless

Mercury

Quicksilver

Grey

Grey

Rubble

Silver

Concrete

Castor

Mica

Granite

Foil

Twilight

Gravel

Gunpowder

Storm

Gunmetal

Greystone

Grey

Hematite

Steel

Sterling

Zinc

Hippo

Volcanic Grey

French Grey

Phantom

Evening Shade

Aluminim

Dover Grey

Cobblestone

Shadow

Quarry

Sharkfin

Tundra

Swordfish

Hurricane

Grey Marl

Silver Dollar

Iron Ore

Boulder

Flintstone

Gunsmoke

Armor

Lava Rock

Harbor Grey

Sweatsuit

Grey

Grey

Potassium

Magnesium

Dust

Silverstone

Celeste'

Melancholy

Greyhound

Sharkskin

Tornado

Smoke

Charcoal

Pewter

Slate

Grey Flannel

Graphite

Iron

Lead

Asphalt

Magma

Anthracite

Marquasite

Brimstone

Machine Grey

Banker's Grey

Charcoal

Black

Ebony

Onyx

Fennel

Anise

Noir

Licorice

Raven

Crow

Blackbird

Sambuca

Tar

Black

Black

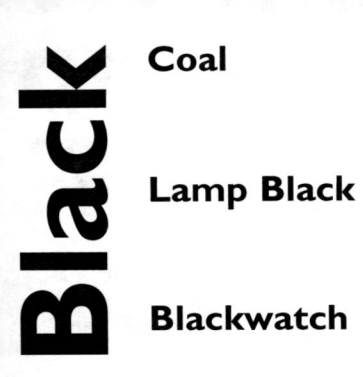

Coal

Lamp Black

Blackwatch

Caviar

Poppy Seed

Rubber

Black Bean

Eclipse

Midnight

Oil

Black Beauty

Tuxedo

Black

Pernod

Black Tie

Nero

Blackjack

Petrol

Eight Ball

Black Ash

Iron Ore

Anisette

Black Russian

Black Pepper

Eel

Multi

Melange

Potpourri

Jambalaya

Tapestry

Rainbow

Cornacopia

Camoflage

Calico

Kaliedoscope

Harlequin

Menagerie

Arabesque

Melding Pot

Multi

www.fashiondex.com

Directories

The Apparel Industry Sourcebook
Reference: 101   **$ 135.00**

Comprehensive directory for apparel manufacturers, designers, merchandisers, trim and fabric buyers and production sourcing departments in the men's, women's, children's and accessory markets.

A complete and up-to-date sourcebook listing over 2,000 nationwide suppliers of all fabrics, trims, notions, forecast services, swatch studios, CAD services and more for the apparel industry.

Listings include:
Company address, phone, fax, email, Sales manager names, Products they sell or manufacture or services they provide. If goods are domestic or imported and where they import from. Minimum quantities for production. Price points, markets they cater to, and more.

Fabric and trim manufacturers, converters, jobbers, agents, mills and reps listed. Over 65 categories serve all your industry sourcing needs.

The Small Design Company's Guide To Wholesale Fabrics
Reference: 106   **$ 65.00**

The perfect sourcebook for companies requiring smaller yardage quantities of production fabric.

This concise directory lists over 400 fabric suppliers selling low minimum (500 yards or less) of a fabric, to the fashion trade. Also listed are suppliers and jobbers of no minimum and in-stock goods.

Listings are grouped by fabric category, and each listing includes company address, phone, fax, email and website address. Also listed is the sales manager name, the fabric qualities they sell, price points, minimum yardage quantities for production, and more!

The sourcebook begins with an excellent introduction chapter which instructs the how-tos' when one is shopping the wholesale fabric market!

Specifically created for start-up companies, small design houses, and home sewing businesses.

*all the info contained in the Small Design Company's Guide is also included in the Apparel Industry Sourcebook.

The Apparel Production Sourcebook American Edition
Reference: 102   **$ 125.00**

An up-to-date directory committed to solving your production sourcing and contracting needs in the Americas.

Hundreds of contractors who are open for production work listed. The sourcebook includes sewing, cut-n-sew, and finishing contractors, along with apparel production and pre-production services from the United States, Canada and South and Central America.

All factories are sorted by clothing classification and by U.S. state or by country. All information is checked two times each year, and is current and up-to-date.

Excellent tool for all production sourcing departments.

Listings include:
Factory Address, Phone, Fax, Email, and Contact Name, Specialty areas, Package capabilities, Machinery, Production Minimums, Sample rooms, Where they export to, And more!

order online: www.fashiondex.com/store or by phone 212 647 0051

Directories

The Apparel Production Sourcebook Asian Edition
Reference: 103 **$ 150.00**

Newly compiled, up-to-date and information-packed directory solves your global production needs! Over 400 apparel and accessory manufacturers, exporters and contractors from 18 Asian countries listed.

Countries include:
China • Bangladesh • Indonesia • India • Korea • Hong Kong • Malaysia • Philippines • Singapore • Pakistan • Thailand • Macau • Taiwan • Sri Lanka

Within each country, manufacturers of all types of woven and knit apparel are listed, and also factories are cross-referenced by product type and by brand name labels they manufacture!

Listings include:
Address, Phone, Fax and Email, Annual sales in US dollars, Payment terms, Lead times, Facility types and amounts, Production capacities, Product types and prices, Minimums for production, Where they export to, Sample rooms and more!

A well-researched and must-have sourcebook for every fashion production department!

Directory of Brand Name Apparel Manufacturers and Importers
Reference: 104 **$ 135.00**

The up-to-date and easy-to-use directory listing brand name and private label manufacturers and importers of women's, men's, and children's wear, plus accessory markets.

Developed and targeted for retail store and catalogue buyers to shop the apparel and accessory markets easily.

Over 2,200 brand name labels listed, broken down by each type of apparel classification. No cross-referencing. No legends to consult.

Listings include:
Company address, phone, fax, email, Label names and line types, Showroom and sales rep locations, Whether products are domestic or imported, Types of retailers sold, Key company contact names, Price points, RN numbers, If they do private-label programs and more.

Independent Sales Reps
Reference:501 **$ 185.00**

Up-to-date directory listing apparel and accessory sales representatives who sell to regional department and specialty stores, boutiques, and more. Designed for manufacturers and importers who are seeking an instant sales force in the U.S.A.

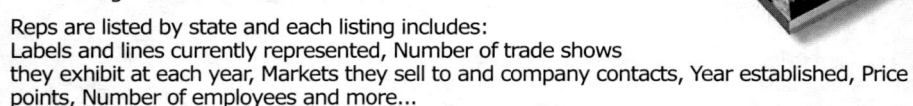

Reps are listed by state and each listing includes:
Labels and lines currently represented, Number of trade shows they exhibit at each year, Markets they sell to and company contacts, Year established, Price points, Number of employees and more...

Sales reps listed are not working for any one company and are looking for new lines for the accounts they currently serve. Finding a good independent sales rep is the first step to profitability!

Fashion Accessories
Reference:502 **$ 130.00**

Great directory that has been created in response to the trend in retail which emphasizes fashion accessories.

order online: www.fashiondex.com/store or by phone 212 647 0051

Directories

The Directory of International Apparel Industry Trade Shows
Reference: 113   **$ 40.00**

Indispensable guide listing over 400 international apparel industry trade shows. Updated directory lists all of the men's, women's and children's apparel shows, plus all textile and trim sourcing shows, apparel technology and production sourcing shows in the U.S.A. and worldwide. Newly updated 2006/2007 edition lists trade shows by name, show type, month in which they occur and continent/country.

Where to Wear Box Set 2006
Reference: 610   **$ 49.95**

The brand new Where to Wear/Box Set 2006 includes four individual books on the shopping meccas of London, Paris, Italy (Rome, Milan and Florence) and New York. Once fashionistas get their hands on it, they will be in retail heaven.

Where to Wear New York Shopping Guide 2006
Reference: 611   **$ 14.95**

Slick, cool and unforgettable, New York City does fashion with sophistication. So, grab this handy directory, and don't miss out on a chance to shop at all the best stores.

Where to Wear Los Angeles Shopping Guide 2006
Reference: 612   **$ 14.95**

No where is it better to see and be seen than in L.A.. Where to Wear Los Angeles covers every shopping hotspot under the L.A. sun, from department stores, to designer flagships, to tiny boutiques.

Where to Wear Florida Shopping Guide 2006
Reference: 661   **$ 14.95**

From the opulence of Palm Beach to the collection of shops at Bal Harbour, Florida boasts one of the greatest concentrations of A-list stores in the world.

Where to Wear London Shopping Guide 2006
Reference: 613   **$ 14.95**

Any fashion follower knows that London is a style mecca and home to some of the most fresh and artistic designers in the world. The 2005 edition of Where to Wear shows visitors where to begin and Londoners where to go next.

Where to Wear Italy Shopping Guide 2006
Reference: 614   **$ 14.95**

Bella Italia. Home to some of the world's most creative and best known designers, Armani, Ferragamo, Gucci and Prada, all have their roots in a country renowned for its luxurious style and sexiness.

order online: www.fashiondex.com/store or by phone 212 647 0051

How To's

Apparel Design and Production Handbook A Technical Reference
Reference: 105   **$ 95.00**

Invaluable reference book for fashion designers, merchandisers, technical designers, production managers, apparel-making factories, patternmakers, and all industry executives working in the men's, women's and children's markets today.

Highlights include:
- How to measure the body for apparel production.
- Standard body measurements for all regular and special sizes of men's, women's & children's wear.
- How to measure garments for apparel production.
- Standard garment specifications and detailed flats for basic woven and knit styles.
- Grading charts for all markets and sizes.
- Blank costing and specification sheets.
- Metric conversion tables.
- Croquis drawings for design, illustration and tracing and more.

The Design Detail Book/Edition 1
Reference: 111   **$ 45.00**
The Design Detail Book/Edition 2
Reference: 112   **$ 45.00**
The Design Detail Book/Edition 1 & 2
Reference: 116   **$ 80.00**

Creative reference book containing an abundance of quick fashion sketches for design development.

Edition One contains all types of garment **necklines, collars, and lapels**, and uniquely illustrates the many possibilities of each detail.

Edition Two contains many more fashion details for design development and features all types of garment **sleeves, cuffs, and shoulders.**

Both books are an excellent source for design inspiration, research and product development. Ideal for fashion designers, merchandisers, costume designers, design room assistants, and more!

The Color Book/Volume One
Reference: 107   **$ 40.00**
The Color Book/Volume Two
Reference: 108   **$ 40.00**
The Color Book/Volume Three
Reference: 114   **$ 40.00**
Set of all Three Color Book Volumes
Reference: 115   **$ 95.00**

We all know the time and mental energy it takes to name colors each season. It's a super-fun part of the job, but often time-consuming and frustrating. With this in mind, we have designed The Color Books to help you name your ranges as quickly as possible, while retaining the level of creativity associated with naming colors.

The Color Book/Volume One
The first edition lists over 1,300 color names. The volume lists color names arranged by hue, and includes all basic colors and the pale and dark shades of each main color.

The Color Book/Volume Two
Volume Two continues the lists of color names, with over 1,000 new, creative and time-saving names. Also included in this edition are names for metallic, transparent, translucent and sparkly colors.

The Color Book/Volume Three
The all new, exciting Volume Three contains 1,200 more super-creative and really fun color names.

Another excellent tool for designers, sales managers, merchandisers, mills, color card makers and catalog companies.

order online: www.fashiondex.com/store or by phone 212 647 0051

How To's

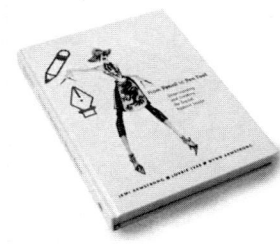

From Pencil To Pen Tool
Understanding & Creating The Digital Fashion Image
Reference: 308   **$ 75.00**

Learn the secrets of Adobe Photoshop and Illustrator!
No longer will fashion professionals and students have to consult bulky computer guidebooks to learn the secrets of Adobe Photoshop and Illustrator!
CD FEATURES • Full-color tutorials • Current croquis • Palettes with preloaded presets of fabric swatches • Library of ready-to-use construction details • Stock photography for fashion graphics • Practice exercises

Rendering Fashion, Fabric and Prints
Reference: 408   **$ 71.00**

Excellent step-by-step guide addressing all aspects of textile and surface design rendering and achieving the desired effects using Adobe PhotoShop. This thorough guide contains descriptions of the various ways to get results, and the best ways for presenting work created in the textile/surface design industry. Accompanying **CD has digital fabric swatch and fabric structure library.**

Fashion Illustration for Designers
Reference: 411 **$ 75.00**

The world of fashion is one of beautiful images and this textbook has been created to teach designers how to draw all types of fashion figures that reflect those beautiful images, in a modern approach. Step-by-step instructions on getting your fashion ideas on paper effectively are detailed. Accompanying **DVD allows viewer to watch actual drawing demonstrations, showing easy-to-learn tecniques**.

Fabric Swatch Kit
Reference: 602   **$ 85.00**

A well-organized fabric collection featuring over 175 swatches for the fashion and textile industries.

Informative and concise, this overview includes all commonly-used fabrics and their uses. Swatches are organized by fabric category, and fabric types are arranged alphabetically in each category.

Simple-to-understand construction details and a technical glossary of terms complete this must-have reference.

Additionally, one gets the opportunity to learn each fabric type as they mount each swatch to its corresponding definition. Loads of extra blank pages are included so you can add your own swatches as well, and build an entire fabric library.

Perfect for everyone in the fashion design and textile trades.

order online: www.fashiondex.com/store or by phone 212 647 0051

Inspiration

Renaissance
Reference: 650   **$ 35.00**

A rich collection of renaissance patterns. Includes free CD-Rom of images.

Traditional Dutch Tile Designs
Reference: 631   **$ 35.00**

Excellent book of Traditional Dutch Tile Design images for use as a graphic resource and for design inspiration. Book includes Dutch tile designs of all types, and includes free CD-Rom of images.

Classical Border Designs
Reference: 630   **$ 35.00**

Great book of images for use as a graphic resource and design inspiration. Book includes Classical Border Designs of all types for design, and includes free CD-Rom of images.

Art Nouveau Design
Reference: 651   **$ 35.00**

A rich collection of art nouveau designs. Includes free CD-Rom of images.

Ancient Mexican Designs
Reference: 670   **$ 35.00**

Excellent book of Ancient Mexican Designs images for use as a graphic resource and for design inspiration. Book includes Ancient Mexican Designs of all types, and includes free CD-Rom of images.

Rococo
Reference: 671   **$ 35.00**

The Rococo is a predominantly French style of the mid-18th century. Both in style and chronologically, Rococo fits in between the boldly ornamental Baroque and the elegant and joyful Romanticism. One the typifying elements of the Rococo is the use of exquisite bouquets as an ornamental detail. includes free CD-Rom of images.

Wallpaper
Reference: 672   **$ 35.00**

Excellent book of Wallpaper Designs images for use as a graphic resource and for design inspiration. Book includes Wallpaper Designs of all types, and includes free CD-Rom of images.

1930's
Reference: 673   **$ 35.00**

Excellent book of 1930's Designs images for use as a graphic resource and for design inspiration. Book includes 1930's Designs of all types, and includes free CD-Rom of images.

Fancy Designs 1920
Reference: 674   **$ 35.00**

Excellent book of Fancy Designs 1920 images for use as a graphic resource and for design inspiration. Book includes Fancy Designs 1920 of all types, and includes free CD-Rom of images.

order online: www.fashiondex.com/store or by phone 212 647 0051

Technical

Quality Assurance for Textiles and Apparel
Reference: 302   **$ 62.00**

Extremely important textbook based on the premise that quality is built into the product from conception to delivery to the consumer. Learn to understand and determine quality and consistency among products. Explains materials testing and evaluating of fiber, textiles, garments, color, durability and more. Details creating standards and specifications, inspecting finished products, sampling a production lot, developing acceptance levels and more. Essential reference on quality for the specific needs and expectations of today's markets.

Fashion Production Terms
Reference: 303   **$ 55.00**

A comprehensive reference book defining over 600 fashion construction terms in detail. All production terms used in garment development through to the finished product are explained. Chapters focus on: draping, drafting, fabric structure, cutting, basting, facings, hems, pressing, seam finishings, supplies, equipment and more. Every term is illustrated with a photograph or drawing. An outstanding source of reference for every individual in or entering the apparel industry.

Sewing for the Apparel Industry
Reference: 406   **$ 80.00**

A detailed workbook focusing on the fundamental principles of garment construction, sewing methods, and all of the assembly elements a designer must consider at the beginning of the design phase. Workbook describes each application in detail with step-by-step directions. Teaches sewing techniques, tailoring, draping, flat patternmaking and how to solve production problems, and more. Introduces production applications based on frequency of use and degree of difficulty. And much more.....

Draping for Fashion Design/Fourth Edition
Reference: 410   **$ 69.00**

Draping for Fashion Design is the definitive basic instructional text for draping. This book covers all of the fundamental instruction and material for beginning and for advanced drapers. Based on current fashion-industry methods, this well layed-out book reflects the dramatic changes of computer integration into the basic design and pattern development process and demonstrates simplified methods wherever they are employed in the industry.

Machine Knitting
Reference: 413   **$ 50.00**

Machine Knitting presents comprehensive instructions for knitting techniques and constructions. Concise, step-by-step directions enhanced by over **300 photos and by animations on the accompanying DVD,** give beginning and advanced machine knitters a complete guide to the procedures and processes of machine knitting.

order online: www.fashiondex.com/store or by phone 212 647 0051

Dictionaries

International Dictionary of Fashion Apparel Terminology in 8 Languages
Reference: 110 $ 39.00

The idea for The International Dictionary of Fashion came when we were traveling in Hong Kong, and could not make ourselves understood either to the Hong Kong factory agent or to the Japanese buyer who was also visiting. It was frustrating, and we went out and purchased two large translation dictionaries, one in each language. Well, that worked, but the books were heavy and did not have enough apparel-related words in their pages. We wished there was just one volume, and that we could look up the words and point to them, in whichever language we needed. So, we thought, "Here's a book idea!".

With that, we compiled our word list and started the book. The word list is a list of over 2,100 words and terms that fashion design professionals need when communicating with other countries.

We included precise names of: style details, garment parts, fabric names, trimmings, notions, structural components, body parts, numbers, colors, and sentences commonly used in fashion design development and production.

The sentence section is an invaluable quick reference addendum. So, if a reader needs to say, **"It's the wrong fabric."** they can express that exactly. This excellent dictionary combines eight different languages into one volume, all for one specific industry.

Languages included: **English, Spanish, French, German, Italian, Chinese, Japanese, Korean**

Fairchild's Dictionary of Textile Terms
Reference: 304 $ 55.00

The industry standard for textile information contains over 14,000 definitions in a revised and expanded 7th edition.

Easy-to-read and understand definitions of all words, terms and common expressions relating to textiles.

Definitions include the technical, aesthetic, historic, geographic and scientific. Pronunciations included for important terms and hundreds of illustrations included.

An invaluable reference for everyone in the apparel, textile and related industries.

Fairchild's Dictionary of Fashion Terms
Reference: 305 $ 55.00

The most comprehensive fashion resource dictionary available listing over 15,000 definitions of all fashion terms.

All clothing terminology explained, plus worldwide fashion fads, trends, styles, business and technology terms defined. Enlightening definitions include the historical and contemporary. Hundreds of illustrations included.

Indispensable tool for the fashion trade.

order online: www.fashiondex.com/store or by phone 212 647 0051

Business

Birnbaum's Global Guide To Winning The Great Garment War
by David Birnbaum
Reference: 201   **$ 35.00**

The premier book on garment costing, and the ultimate book for all garment industry professionals. Ideal for buyers, suppliers, manufacturers and all those working to develop an apparel export industry in any country. This great text details all the different cost factors that go into a garment, and how to get the best price and work with the lowest cost. With humor and wit, David Birnbaum uses his lifetime of experience in the international garment trade to answer all the following questions:

HOW do you buy at the lowest cost?
HOW do you produce at the lowest cost?
HOW can you compete internationally?
HOW do you decide which country to source product from?
HOW do you decide which factory to work with?

Birnbaum's Global Guide To Material Sourcing
by David Birnbaum
Reference: 220   **$ 45.00**

The global garment industry is moving from product supplier to service provider. This great, new text by David Birnbaum explains how to source fabric and trims in the post-2005 era. You can no longer depend on how you sourced materials a few years ago, those methods are already antiquated. Is your company on the leading edge, or are you falling behind? Sourcing-expert David Birnbaum answers these questions and more.

How can your factory move from being just one more garment maker to be becoming an irreplaceable asset in your customer's supply chain? How can you the importer reduce costs and at the same time gain greater speed-to-market by transferring the processes to your overseas supplier? 70% of FOB price is material: How do you find the materials you need, for the delivery you need, and at the price you want? The quota phase out has changed the garment industry forever. To remain competitive, factories will have to provide more services and customers will have to reduce their overheads by pushing the process to the factory. Whether you are a retailer, importer, factory or agent, unless you've read this book, you are falling behind

The Birnbaum Report Strategic Sourcing for Garment Importers
by David Birnbaum
Reference: 204   **$ 400.00/12 issues**

A monthly electronic newsletter by David Birnbaum, detailing all the news and trends in the international garment industry, to help manufacturers and importers work at the best price and source in the best countries.

Researched and written by David Birnbaum. He applies his lifetime of outstanding experience working in the international garment-industry sourcing trade each month, so that the reader will be able to make knowledgeable decisions about their future production sourcing plans.

The newsletter is geared to manufacturers, importers, retail buyers, factories, agents, and government and non-government organizations. The newsletter will analyze all that is happening in this great period of garment-industry-sourcing change.

order online: www.fashiondex.com/store or by phone 212 647 0051

Business

The Vendor Compliance Handbook
Reference: 222   **$ 95.00**

This book outlines everything a designer or a garment manufacturer needs to know about producing a garment from start to finish. The book includes all the steps they can perform to avoid disconcerting incidents, such as chargebacks and late deliveries

This book illustrates what it is that makes a designer succeed, as well as ways to make a production office run more smoothly. It outlines the way to manufacture a garment from the development of a sales sample to shipping the finished garment on time, and all of the "how to's" in between. The book demonstrates how to apply these ideas to an existing organization or to a start-up company. The book is ideal for the young designer, who is looking to begin a business, or for an existing company, that is having trouble with anything from poor or inconsistent fit to late shipping and charge backs. Included in the book are examples of forms and templates that you can compare to your existing ones. Together with this, it gives you a sample plan and action calendar that will help with your organization of all the development stages. All these forms will be useful when comparing them with your existing ones to see where you may be going wrong.

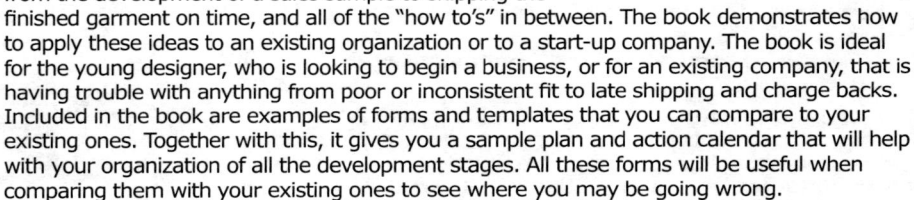

The Business of Fashion
Designing, Manufacturing, and Marketing
Reference: 301   **$ 88.00**

This heavily illustrated textbook focuses on the organization and operation of the fashion industry and how apparel is designed, manufactured, marketed and distributed. Includes structure of the U.S. textile and apparel industries, legal framework, ready-to-wear company organization and more. Explains the processes of design development, style selecting and marketing. Encompasses preproduction, production, sourcing, quality assurance, distribution and retailing. Captures the true dynamics of the fashion industry's many components.

Ready-to-Wear Apparel Analysis
Reference: 405   **$ 85.00**

Excellent reference guide that concisely covers all areas of apparel design, evaluation, production and merchandising. Chapters, in this third edition, define the processes of mass garment production, design development, evaluation of cost, the priority of quality, government regulations, labeling, garment assembly, stitch types, seam types, related vocabulary and much, much more. Equally useful to beginners as well as experienced industry professionals.

Apparel Manufacturing/Sewn Product Analysis
Reference: 407   **$ 89.00**

This comprehensive textbook provides in-depth coverage of all facets of apparel manufacturing in today"s global industry.
This is an extremely useful reference manual for students and executives alike in the fashion manufacturing industry. Details the organization of the apparel business, and the complexities in working in our worldwide market; all of the apparel development and technical design processes; apparel quality, cost and sourcing; and production processes, planning, and management decisions.

order online: www.fashiondex.com/store or by phone 212 647 0051

Business

Fashion For Profit
Reference: 601   **$ 55.00**

What do you need to do in order to get those creative, hot ideas into a finished product, and into the stores?

If you want to know how to start your own fashion company, Fashion for Profit has all the answers of these questions and more:
How much money will I need to start my own business? Where will I find the funds to support my venture? What licenses do I need? How do I put a business plan together? How do I cost a garment and make a profit? How do I sell to the retailers?.

Fashion For Profit Seminar/Two-hour DVD
Reference: 606   **$ 25.00**

A great compliment to the book Fashion for Profit, author Frances Harder brings together fashion-industry experts for a two-hour seminar and an informative round-table discussion. We are fortunate to have taped this recent seminar which we are making available to you here.

Costing For Profit
Reference: 657   **$ 19.99**

Every entrepreneur's ultmate goal is to run a successful company. Understanding the complexity of how to cost effectively will play a major part in achieving this goal.

Forms For Profit CD
Reference: 669   **$ 19.99**

Invoices, costing sheets, sales order forms have been built in a dynamic format so calculations can be achieved in Microsoft Excel. Sales Order Forms, Order Confirmation, Invoice, Cutting Ticket, Bill of Materials, Pick Ticket , Purchase Order, Packing Slips , Cost Sheets, Pattern Card, Specification Sheets, Sales Rep Agreement, Contractors Agreement, Credit Check Application and More...

Fashion Designers Survival Guide
Reference: 646   **$ 22.95**

Provides the necessary tools to get a fashion line or label up and moving on the right track, including: Start-up costs and financing Legal issues Business plans Public relations and sales Marketing and manufacturing Distribution-trade, trunk, and runway shows.

The Official Step By Step Guide to Starting a Clothing Line
Reference: 648   **$ 44.95**

This is the manual that will help you launch your clothing line in a big way like a pro! This guide is a very informative step by step manual that educates aspiring designers on how to create their own clothing line from scratch. It covers everything you need to know and more!

order online: www.fashiondex.com/store or by phone 212 647 0051

Patternmaking

The Practical Guide To Patternmaking For Fashion Designers: Menswear
Reference: 306 $ 70.00

The Practical Guide to Patternmaking for Fashion Designers: Menswear offers patternmaking techniques for a variety of garment styles and includes information on sizing, lining, and a variety of fabrics. Covering everything from casual to tailored designs, it can serve both as an introduction to the pattern-drafting skills necessary for menswear and as a more in-depth treatment of patternmaking techniques. The guide covers the patternmaking process for an array of menswear garments, as well as the accompanying theories and concepts.

The Practical Guide To Patternmaking For Fashion Designers: Juniors, Misses and Women
Reference: 307 $ 90.00

The Practical Guide to Patternmaking for Fashion Designers: Juniors, Misses, and Women offers an in-depth look into the techniques and theories of pattern drafting for women's garments. Covering a wide variety of styles, textiles, and sizes, this book is useful for a wide range of pattern courses from introductory to advanced. It provides a sound introduction to the concepts and the processes of patternmaking, as well as a more advanced analysis of style and design. The book offers helpful techniques on taking measurements and adjusting the fit of garments for all body sizes, patterns, and types of fabrics.

Patternmaking
Reference: 409 $ 74.00

This comprehensive text covers all the technical aspects of developing precise professional patterns for garments, and gives a firm foundation in the tools, concepts, and methods necessary for success in this highly competitive industry.

Patternmaking for Fashion Design
Reference: 415 $ 92.00

This quintessential guide to patternmaking offers comprehensive coverage, clear illustrations and easy-to-follow instructions, providing users with all the relevant information necessary to create design patterns with accuracy regardless of their complexity. Covers the three steps in the development of design patterns—dart manipulation, added fullness, and contouring—with a central theme that all designs are based on one, or more of these three major patternmaking and design principles. Includes a fashion sketch for each project with an analysis of the design, and focuses on pattern plot and manipulation for developing the patterns. Illustrates several methods for knock-offs, and dedicates new sections on fitting corrections for the basic pattern set and the four pant foundation; menswear; patternmaking for bias-cut garments; revised drafting instructions and standard measurement charts; how to modify the bodice to fit the different sizes of bust cups; constructed support for strapless designs, and more. Presents additional and more challenging design projects for the advanced reader. For dressmakers, home sewers, manufacturing companies, and professionals in fashion design and fashion merchandising.

order online: www.fashiondex.com/store or by phone 212 647 0051

#	Title	Price
001	Sourcing Made Simpler/On-line Access	205.00 _____
101	Apparel Industry Sourcebook	135.00 _____
102	Apparel Production Sourcebook (American Edition)	125.00 _____
103	Apparel Production Sourcebook (Asian Edition)	150.00 _____
104	Directory of Brand Name Apparel Manufacturers and Importers	135.00 _____
105	Apparel Design and Production Handbook/A Technical Reference	95.00 _____
106	The Small Design Company's Guide To Wholesale Fabrics	65.00 _____
107	Color Book/Volume I	40.00 _____
108	Color Book/Volume II	40.00 _____
110	Intl. Dictionary of Fashion/Apparel Terminology in 8 Languages	39.00 _____
111	The Design Detail Book/Edition 1:	45.00 _____
112	The Design Detail Book/Edition 2:	45.00 _____
113	The Directory of International Apparel Industry Trade Shows	40.00 _____
114	Color Book/Volume III	40.00 _____
115	Color Book/Volume I, II, III	95.00 _____
116	The Design Detail Book/Edition 1 and 2	80.00 _____
117	A Designer's Book of Bridal Gowns by Debby Roosa	40.00 _____
201	Birnbaum's Global Guide To Winning The Great Garment War	35.00 _____
204	The Birnbaum Report/Strategic Sourcing for Garment Importers	400.00 _____
220	Birnbaum's Global Guide To Material Sourcing	45.00 _____
221	Birnbaum's Annual Report of Garment Imports 2005	65.00 _____
222	The Vendor Compliance Handbook	95.00 _____
301	The Business of Fashion/Designing, Manufacturing, and Marketing	88.00 _____
302	Quality Assurance for Textiles and Apparel	62.00 _____
303	Fashion Production Terms	55.00 _____
304	Dictionary of Textile Terms	55.00 _____
305	Dictionary of Fashion Terms	55.00 _____
306	The Practical Guide To Patternmaking: Menswear	70.00 _____
307	The Practical Guide To Patternmaking: Juniors, Misses and Women	90.00 _____
308	From Pencil To Pen Tool	75.00 _____
405	Ready-to-Wear Apparel Analysis	85.00 _____
406	Sewing for the Apparel Industry	80.00 _____
407	Apparel Manufacturing/Sewn Product Analysis	89.00 _____
408	Rendering Fashion, Fabric and Prints	71.00 _____
409	Patternmaking	74.00 _____
410	Draping for Fashion Design/Fourth Edition	69.00 _____
411	Fashion Illustration for Designers	75.00 _____
412	9 Heads	90.00 _____
413	Machine Knitting	50.00 _____
415	Patternmaking for Fashion Design	92.00 _____
501	Independent Sales Reps	185.00 _____
502	Fashion Accessories	130.00 _____
601	Fashion For Profit	55.00 _____
602	Fabric Swatch Kit	85.00 _____
603	Computer-Aided Flat Sketching for the Fashion Industry	45.00 _____
604	Applied Flat Sketching for the Fashion Industry	30.00 _____
605	Flat Sketching for the Fashion Industry	25.00 _____

order online: www.fashiondex.com/store or by phone 212 647 0051

606	Fashion For Profit Seminar/Two-hour DVD	25.00	_____
610	Where to Wear/2006 Box Set	49.95	_____
611	Where to Wear/New York Shopping Guide	14.95	_____
612	Where to Wear/Los Angeles Shopping Guide	14.95	_____
613	Where to Wear/London Shopping Guide	14.95	_____
614	Where to Wear/Italy Shopping Guide	14.95	_____
615	Where to Wear/Paris Shopping Guide	14.95	_____
616	Tudor Designs	15.00	_____
617	Native American Designs	15.00	_____
619	Art Nouveau Designs	15.00	_____
620	Aztec Designs	15.00	_____
621	Celtic Knotwork Designs	15.00	_____
630	Classical Border Designs	35.00	_____
631	Traditional Dutch Tile Designs	35.00	_____
634	Textiles at Temple Newsam	35.00	_____
636	Decorated Paper Designs	30.00	_____
637	Fashion in Film	19.95	_____
639	Batik Designs	30.00	_____
646	Fashion Designers Survival Guide	22.95	_____
648	The Official Step By Step Guide to Starting a Clothing Line.	44.95	_____
650	Renaissance	35.00	_____
651	Art Nouveau Designs	35.00	_____
657	Costing For Profit	19.99	_____
661	Where to Wear/Florida	14.95	_____
662	Where to Wear/Las Vegas Shopping Guide	14.95	_____
669	Forms for Profit	19.99	_____
670	Ancient Mexican Designs	35.00	_____
671	Rococo	35.00	_____
672	Wallpaper	35.00	_____
673	1930's	35.00	_____
675	Japanese Patterns	35.00	_____

Sub Total _____
(1/book 8.00, 2/books 12.00, 3+/books 16.00) .... Shipping _____
Tax NY only (%8.375) _____
Total _____

Name on Credit Card...
Credit Card Number .... C V V# _____ Exp. Date _____
Ship To:
    Company: ....
    Name:..
    Address:..
    City/State/Zip:..
    Email ....
    Phone..
Shipping & handling add $ 8.00/12.00/16.00, Outside USA please check website for rates.
New York State orders add 8.375% tax.
Price subject to change.
ALL INFORMATION PROVIDED IS SUBJECT TO CHANGE WITHOUT NOTICE
order online: www.fashiondex.com/store or by phone 212 647 0051

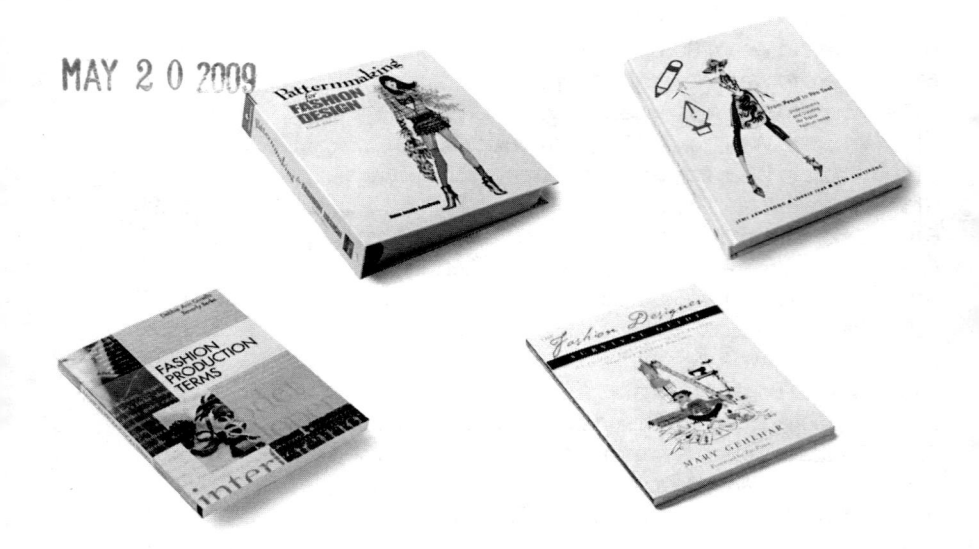

THE FASHIONDEX, INC.
Showroom • 153 West 27th Street • Suite 701 • New York, NY 10001
Corporate Office • 136 Colabaugh Road • 3rd Fl • Croton on Hudson, NY 10520
212 647 0051 • 914 271 6121 • 877 647 0051 • Fax 914 271 6302
info@fashiondex.com
Order Online at www.fashiondex.com/store/

www.fashiondex.com/store